KU-420-311

Awesome Facts
about

Volcanoes

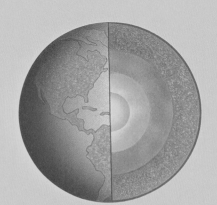

Clare Oliver

Aladdin / Watts
London • Sydney

Contents

Awesome Facts about

Volcanoes

C151856093

This edition published in 2001
© Aladdin Books Ltd 1998
Produced by
Aladdin Books Ltd
28 Percy Street
London W1P 0LD

ISBN 0-7496-4243-2 (paperback)

Previously published in hardcover
in the series "I Didn't Know That"
ISBN 0-7496-3248-8 (hardback)

First published in Great Britain in 1998 by
Aladdin Books/Watts Books
96 Leonard Street
London EC2A 4XD

Editor: Liz White
Design: David West Children's Books
Designer: Flick Killerby
Illustrators: Ian Thompson, Peter Roberts - Allied Artists,
Jo Moore

Printed in the U.A.E.

All rights reserved
A CIP catalogue record for this book is available from
the British Library

**KENT
ARTS & LIBRARIES**

C151856093

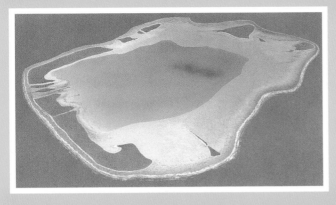

Introduction

Did *you* know that most volcanoes are under the sea? ... that vulcanologists are volcano scientists? ... that the biggest volcano is on Mars?

Discover for yourself amazing facts about the Earth's volcanoes and the people who study them. Learn about tsunamis, hot springs, black smokers and about volcanoes of the past – and in space.

Look out for this symbol which means there is a fun project for you to try.

Is it true or is it false? Watch for this symbol and try to answer the question before reading on for the answer.

 Copy the map of the Earth below, or blow it up on a photocopier. Colour it in, then cut along the fault lines. Can you fit all the plates back together? Can you find the Pacific Ocean plate? There are so many volcanoes around this plate that the area is called the Ring of Fire.

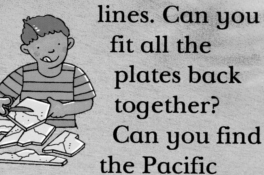

Most earthquakes are not even noticeable, but about every three years there is a violent one somewhere in the world. In 1970 an earthquake in Peru made roads crack and buildings collapse. It caused a massive landslide – and 66,000 deaths.

On the surface

The San Andreas fault in California, on the West Coast of the United States, is where two plates are sliding past each other in opposite directions. There have been lots of big earthquakes along this line. Even so, many people make their homes there.

The Earth's *crust* is made of pieces called *plates*. These don't join up neatly, some overlap, and there are gaps between others. Volcanoes and earthquakes usually happen at *fault lines* where the edges of plates move apart or grate together.

The slow movement of fault lines is measured with a creepmeter!

Cracking up

Volcanoes are openings in the Earth's crust, often on a fault line. Rock below the Earth's surface can get so hot it forms *magma*. When the pressure rises it blasts a hole and the hot melted rock, ash and gas escape.

Geysers (above) are openings in the Earth which shoot out fountains of boiling water. Volcanic heat boils up water that is trapped underground.

Crater

Pipe

Dyke

Cone

Volcanoes are named after Vulcan, Roman god of fire and metalwork.

There is fire at the centre of the Earth.

Outer core (liquid metal)

Inner core (solid metal)

Outer mantle (hot rock)

Inner mantle (hot rock)

Answer: **False**

Long ago people believed that a fire inside our planet gave all volcanoes their fiery power. Now we know the Earth's *core* is metal, and that a hot *mantle* of rock surrounds the core.

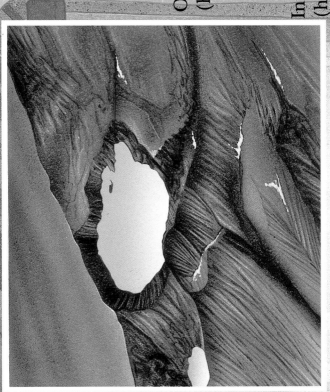

Vent

Magma chamber

When they erupt, volcanoes really blow their top! They leave a *crater*. If it's really big it's called a *caldera*. The one above is on the Japanese volcano, Shirane. It's so long since Shirane erupted that its crater has filled with rainwater and become a lake.

Rivers of rock

When a volcano erupts, it squirts out hot, liquid rock called *lava*. Sometimes the lava is treacly and just oozes out. Sometimes the lava is so runny it gushes in rivers, flowing at speeds up to 50 km/h.

When a volcano shoots lava into the air it makes a fountain of fire which can reach 100 m in height. Molten rock can also come out as house-sized lava bombs, little stones called lapilli, or clouds of ash and dust.

Pumice stone is hardened lava - it can help to soften your feet!

Very fluid lava plops to Earth like a cowpat.

True or false?
Lava has skin.

Answer: **True**
Pahoehoe (pa hoy hoy) is a very hot, fluid type of lava that grows a smooth skin on top as it cools. The hot flow continues underneath, even though the crust may be hard enough to walk across.

 SEARCH & FIND Can you find five lava bombs? FIND SEARCH &

 Warning – adult help needed!
Make an *eruption*! Half-fill a jar with bicarbonate of soda. Cut a circle out of card. Make a slit to the middle and tape into a cone shape. Cut a hole at the top of the cone and place over the jar. Add some red food colouring to vinegar. Pour it into the jar, then stand back! This can be messy. Wear old clothes and do it outdoors!

True or false?
There really is a blue moon.

Answer: **True**

Floating clouds of volcanic ash do strange things to light. They can even make the Moon and Sun seem to glow blue or green!

The static in an ash cloud can also make lightning. To make static, put a metal tray on a plastic bag. Fix a plasticine 'handle' on the tray, then rub it around on the bag. Lift the tray and, with your other hand, touch its edge with a metal fork to see sparks fly!

Volcanic ash is good for crops - in small amounts!

Spitting ash

Violent volcanoes blast out ash and gas. The force of Mount St. Helens' eruption in 1980 was as powerful as 500 atomic bombs going off. The cloud gave amazing red sunsets and ash fell over 1,200 km away in Colorado.

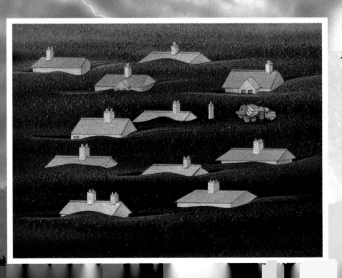

Ash clouds can block out the Sun for days. In 1973, the cloud from an eruption on Heimaey (left), off Iceland, left behind a thick blanket of black ash. In some places the ash was over 6 m deep.

Time freezer

Ash from volcanoes can freeze people in time! In AD 79 Mount Vesuvius split open and a huge glowing cloud billowed out. 2,000 people in Pompeii were buried in the blizzard of ash.

Pliny the Elder died in the eruption. His nephew wrote about the event – that's how we know about what happened.

SEARCH & FIND & FIND SEARCH & FIND

Can you find the bowl of figs?

14

Pompeii lay forgotten for 1,600 years. Another eruption uncovered the original town. The bodies had decayed leaving people-shaped holes in the hardened ash. By filling these moulds with plaster of Paris, archaeologists made models of the Romans – and their pets!

SEARCH & FIND & SEARCH & FIND & Can you find four palm trees?

Making waves

Erupting volcanoes can start tidal waves or *tsunamis* up to 30 m high. After the biggest-ever volcanic eruption, at Krakatoa, 36,000 people were drowned in huge black walls of water.

True or false?
Tsunamis are always caused by volcanoes.

Answer: **False**
Tsunamis happen after earthquakes, too. Tsunamis following the Chilean earthquake in 1960 were so powerful that they toppled the statues on Easter Island.

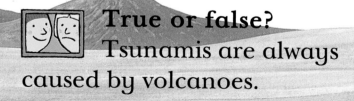

The Berouw (above) was pitched 2.6 km upriver by the Krakatoa tsunami in 1883. It is still there today.

The artist Hokusai painted a very famous picture of a tsunami. Called *The Great Wave*, it shows an enormous tsunami in front of the Japanese volcano Mount Fujiyama which is actually 3,776 m high.

Tsunami is Japanese for 'wave breaking in the harbour'.

SEARCH & FIND & SEARCH & FIND

Can you find three fulmars?

Iceland is a land of fire and ice, with several active volcanoes and geysers. It formed over millions of years from volcanic eruptions in the Mid-Atlantic Ridge. It is over 50,000 times bigger than Surtsey.

Island builders

If enough lava builds around an underwater volcano it will stick out of the sea, making an island. This is how the island of Surtsey was formed in the Icelandic Sea. Surtsey appeared in 1963. By 1967 it measured 1.9 km across.

By 1970 a fulmar had nested on Surtsey and soon flowers took root. Their seeds were carried from Iceland in bird droppings.

! The world's newest island appeared near Tonga in 1995.

Underwater smokers

The world's longest mountain range is the Mid-Atlantic Ridge, a string of volcanoes under water. Submersibles such as *Alvin* go down and take photographs of it.

The seabed surrounding an underwater volcano is an amazing place. *Black smokers* are formed when hot springs on the seabed gush out water that is black with metals.

The metals harden in the cold water, forming tall chimneys.

Alvin

True or false?

There are pillows on the sea bed.

Answer: True

Underwater volcanoes erupt slowly because of the weight of the water. Their lava cools to form lumps called pillows.

The black smokers leak out poisonous sulphur. Even so, giant tube worms (left) live in the pitch-black water around them, feeding on the sulphur-rich bacteria there.

Swarms of shrimp feed around the chimneys on the bacteria in the water. A spot on their back can detect the glow given out by the black smokers.

Most of the Earth's volcanoes are under the sea.

Mud bath

Some people like taking baths in mud! Volcanic heat underground can cause hot springs and bubbling mud pools. Though some pools are boiling hot and would scald your skin, others are cool enough to bathe in. People wallow in the warm mud. The minerals in the mud leave skin feeling soft and smooth.

The Japanese town of Beppu has 4,000 hot springs all to itself. The Jungle Bath (above), at over 6,000 sq m, is the biggest spa in the world.

The Romans believed that spas had healing powers.

 True or false?
Volcanoes have healing powers.

Answer: **True**

It can't be proven, but lots of people believe they do! In Japan, people like to get up to their necks in warm volcanic sand (left). They believe it can cure illnesses. Drinking mineral-rich water from hot springs is thought to keep the body healthy and bathing in hot springs soothes pain.

SEARCH & FIND & FIND & SEARCH

Can you find the swimming cap?

Sleeping mountains

Between eruptions, volcanoes sleep, or are *dormant*. Sometimes they are dormant for centuries. In France are remains of *extinct* volcanoes. The *cone* weathers away but the hard vent is left. It is hard to be sure a volcano is really extinct.

Nogorongoro, an extinct volcano in Tanzania (right), is home to flamingoes and hippos. Its crater is a lake and the lush grassland around it feeds rhinos and zebras.

True or false?
Volcanoes make money.

Answer: **True**

They provide us with precious and useful minerals which formed millions of years ago in the hardening lava. This South African diamond mine (right) at Kimberley is on the site of an extinct volcano.

Two volcanoes that erupted in Turkey eight million years ago have long disappeared. But the lava left behind a 'city' of fairytale cones, into which people dug houses and churches that can still be seen today.

A volcano's remains at Le Puy, France

! To keep volcanoes dormant, the Aztecs fed them women.

True or false?

The largest volcano is in space.

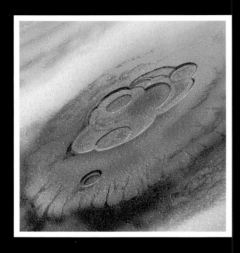

Answer: **True**
The largest known volcano isn't on Earth at all! Mars is home to Olympus Mons, which is 600 km across and 25 km high. Like all Mars' volcanoes, Olympus Mons is extinct.

Space volcanoes

Our planet is not the only place where volcanoes are found. One of Jupiter's moons, Io, is covered in erupting volcanoes. The two *Voyager* spacecraft sent back photographs of the volcanic gas plumes there – which were higher than 30 Mount Everests!

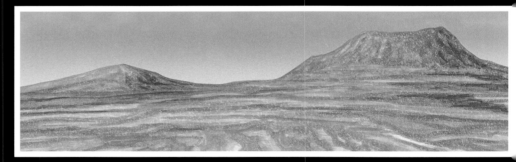

Nearer home, there are volcanoes on our Moon, and on Mars and Venus. The *Magellan* spacecraft used radar to take pictures of Venus' volcanoes.

The volcanoes on Venus may still be active.

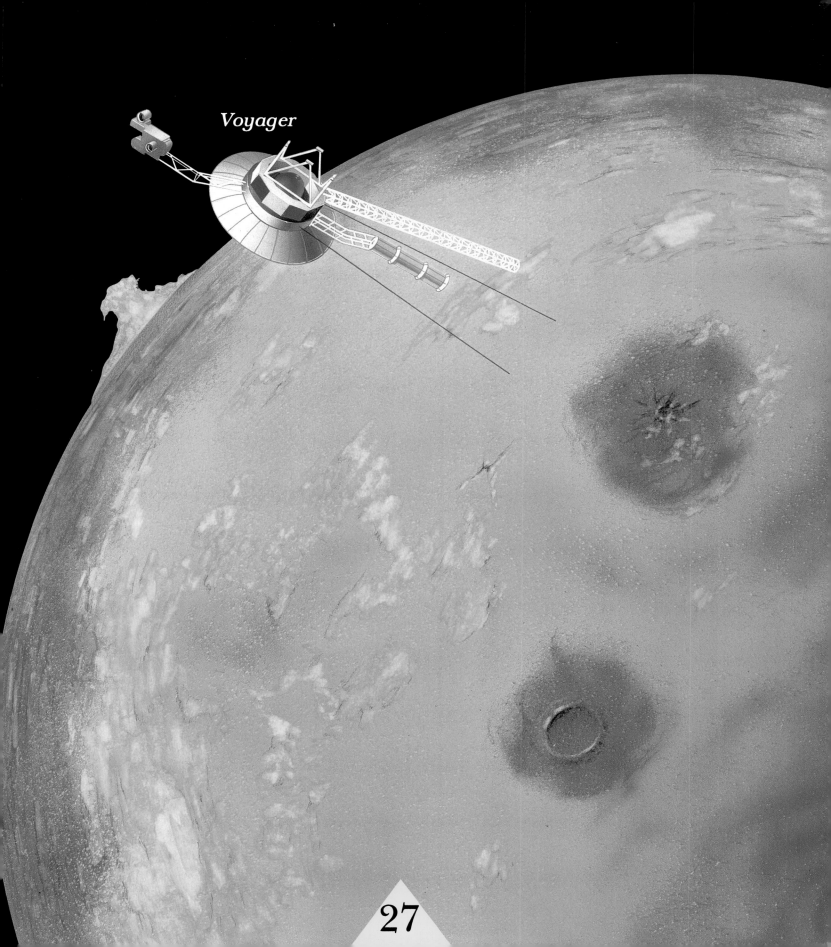

Hot work

Volcanoes are so hot that the people who study them need special protection. *Vulcanologists* wear silver clothing, like a space suit, which reflects the heat. Vulcanologists can monitor a volcano's activity by taking its temperature and collecting samples.

A compass will not work near a volcano. A volcano has its own magnetic force which confuses the compass and makes it go berserk. Hold a magnet next to a compass and see what happens.

Vulcanologists now monitor 50 of the world's active volcanoes.

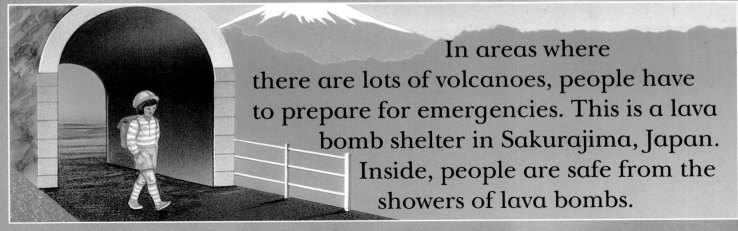

In areas where there are lots of volcanoes, people have to prepare for emergencies. This is a lava bomb shelter in Sakurajima, Japan. Inside, people are safe from the showers of lava bombs.

Vulcanologists take samples of lava to examine in the laboratory. They swirl a long pole into the flow to collect it — just like candy floss collects around its wooden stick.

Vulcanologists wear gas masks so they don't breathe in poisonous gases, or choke on ash. Finding out about volcanoes is a dangerous job. When vulcanologists can forecast eruptions, they can save lives.

Glossary

Black smoker
A hot spring on the ocean bed.

Caldera
A huge volcanic crater, formed when the slopes of a volcano collapse into the empty magma chamber.

Cone
The 'mountain' of hardened lava that builds up around a volcano.

Core
The centre of the Earth.

Crater
The bowl-shaped hollow at the top of a volcano, above the vent.

Crust
The outer layer of the Earth.

Dormant
A volcano is dormant, or sleeping, between eruptions.

Eruption
The way a volcano throws out gases, rocks and ash onto the Earth's surface.

Extinct
A volcano is extinct when it is never going to erupt again.

Fault line
A crack in the Earth's crust.

Geyser
A fountain of water heated by volcanic activity underground.

Lava
Magma that has reached the Earth's surface. It cools as flows on land or pillows under the sea.

Magma
Hot molten rock, which is still below the Earth's surface.

Mantle
The hot layer of earth between the Earth's crust and the Earth's core.

Plates
Large sections of the Earth's crust which are constantly moving against each other.

Tsunami
A giant wave, caused by a volcanic eruption or an earthquake.

Vulcanologist
Someone who studies volcanoes.

Index

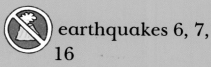
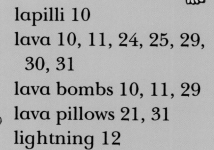